Easy Rambles

around

Keswick & Borrowdale

Vivienne Crow

Questa

ISBN 978-1-898808-26-8

Maps:

The maps accompanying the walks in this book are purely diagram-matic, and are based on maps produced by Harvey Map Services Ltd (Licence No. 75930 © Harvey Map Services Ltd.)

Published by
Questa Publishing Limited
27 Camwood, Clayton-le-Woods,
Bamber Bridge,
Lancashire PR5 8LA

CONTENTS

NOTE

The routes, none of which is more than a 10-minute drive or bus/boat trip from Keswick, are in ascending order of difficulty. Some keep to the valley floor, following idyllic farm and lakeshore paths; some seek out the beautiful views that can be had from the tracks skirting the lower slopes of the mountains; others head on to the easily accessible tops of the low-lying fells. But all of them provide relaxing walking in some of the most beautiful scenery in the British Isles.

Apart from the above, no attempt has been made to grade the walks, as this is too subjective. Use the information about distance and height gain to calculate how long the walk will take.

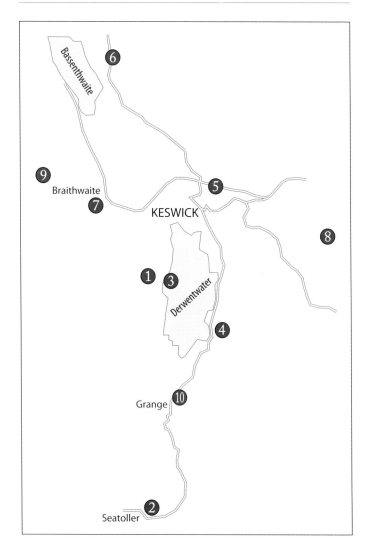

INTRODUCTION

Keswick and Borrowdale are a paradise for anyone who enjoys walking – whether they want to reach the tops of the mountains or are happy to stay at lower levels. With sparkling lakes sitting serenely in spectacularly carved valleys, long rugged ridges endowed with amazing panoramas, jagged crags hanging from grand summits, sweeping dales cradling remote hamlets and lonely fells tonsured with the remains of centuries-old mine workings, this area of the northern Lake District has everything that a lover of the great outdoors could desire.

The mountains here are among the oldest in the world, the Skiddaw slates having been laid down by sedimentary processes more than 450 million years ago. Hardened and compressed on the sea bed, these tend to give us steep, smooth, rounded fells. The Borrowdale volcanics, on the other hand, lend themselves to a rougher, more angular landscape.

The Lake District is essentially a massive volcanic dome fissured by tectonic forces and then sculpted by glaciation to create a spray of valleys and dividing mountain ranges radiating from a central hub like the spokes of a wheel. Much of what we see today was created during the ice ages. The glaciers gouged out deep valleys and corries that are now home to high-level tarns. Hanging valleys, knife-edge arêtes, waterfalls and valley heads filled with drumlin fields – these typical, often dramatic Lake District features are all the work of the massive rivers of ice that once smothered this area.

But the influence of man, too, on this beautiful corner of north-west England must never be underestimated. As you marvel at the views from the terrace path below Cat Bells or the summit of Latrigg, remember that these slopes would probably still be cloaked in oak, birch and pine had humans not cleared the forests to use the wood in the smelting industry, to make bobbins for the textile industry or simply to make way for grazing.

Mining has also left its mark. In the 1560s, 50 German miners were brought to Cumberland to work in the mines, centred initially around the

Newlands valley near Keswick, but quickly spreading into neighbouring dales. As you stride out along the spectacular ridge of Barrow or skirt the base of Castle Crag, you will see the legacy of the mining and quarrying industries, now as much a part of the Lake District landscape as the tarns and becks themselves. Today, only one mine remains in operation – the Honister Slate Mine, which was reopened in 1997 by a local businessman.

The modern economy relies mostly on two industries – tourism and agriculture, no longer at loggerheads with each other, but increasingly aware of their interdependence. While tourists provide farmers with a valuable source of alternative income – by staying in the bed and breakfasts they run or buying produce direct from the farm gate – local farmers have become stewards of the very landscape that attracted the tourists in the first place, grazing the fells to keep them clear of dense vegetation and maintaining the hedgerows and drystone walls that adorn the valley floors.

As you wander the northern Lake District, it is hard not to become intrigued by the unusual-sounding names of the mountains and streams. In fact, you won't find the word for mountain – fell – or the word for stream – beck – used in many other parts of the country. And the names of villages and hamlets are generally lacking those dull Anglian suffixes such as –ton and –ham. This is due to the strong Norse influence. It is generally believed that the first Norse settlers came into the area, not directly from Scandinavia, but via Ireland and the Isle of Man some time before the second half of the 9th century.

Look at a map of the area and you will find it is awash with words not unlike those on any modern map of Norway or Iceland – words such as fell (fjell), beck (bekkr) tarn (tjörn) and dale (dalr). The Scandinavian word saeter, meaning summer pasture, can be found in names such as Seatoller (the saeter among the alders) and Seathwaite (the clearing with the saeter). And villages and hamlets carrying the suffix -thwaite (tveit), meaning a clearing or enclosure in the woods, are too many to mention.

Many other place names have their origins in the Celtic languages – the words Cumberland and Cumbria, for example, deriving from the word *cymry*, meaning compatriots. Links with modern Welsh can be seen in elements such as *glyn* (valley), *pen* (head) and *blaen* (top). Again, pick up a map and you'll quickly spot them – Glencoyne, Penrith, Blencathra are just a few.

Despite centuries of human interference, this area of the Lake District remains relatively rich in birdlife. The fell-tops are home all year round to ravens, buzzards and peregrines. Lower down, in the spring, you'll encounter migratory species such as redstart, pied flycatcher, wood warbler and tree pipit as well as the year-round residents, including chaffinch, green and great-spotted woodpeckers, nuthatch and sparrowhawk. You can find waterfowl on Derwentwater and Bassenthwaite Lake, while the rivers and becks are home to dippers, wagtails and common sandpipers. A pair of ospreys recently made the shores of Bassenthwaite Lake their summer fishing ground, returning every April from their winter sojourn under the African sun to their nest in the Lake District.

High fell wildlife includes foxes, hares and stoats. Herds of red deer can often be seen above the treeline, while the woods are home to badgers, roe deer, voles, shrews, occasional otters and the iconic red squirrel, sadly under threat from the incursion of the more dominant American greys into one of their last bastions in England.

Depending on the time of year, it is possible to see any – or even all –of the above birds and mammals on the walks in this book, especially if you are up with the dawn or walking late in the evening.

1

Around Swinside

This gentle stroll along mostly level, well-constructed paths takes you through pretty woodland near Derwentwater and alongside Newlands Beck. Take your time so that you can really appreciate the beautiful surroundings and, hopefully, spot a few woodland birds.

Start/Finish: Small parking area at Gutherscale,
near Skelgill (NY245211).
*Although other walkers do it, please do not park on the road
leading up to Gutherscale as this causes access problems
for local people and the emergency services*
Distance: 7.7km (4.8 miles)
Height gain: 152m (500ft)

---

1. From the car park, turn right along the narrow lane and then left at the T-junction. Cross the cattle grid and, when the road bends sharp left, turn right along a narrow footpath towards Keswick and Hawes End.

2. Cross straight over the next road and go through the pedestrian gate to the left of the Hawes End centre driveway. The well-constructed path, part of both the Cumbria Way and the Allerdale Ramble, heads through attractive woodland and passes close to Lingholm, a large, Victorian house on the shores of Derwentwater.

> *The Lingholm estate is home to a flock of Soay sheep, one of the oldest known breeds in the world. You should be able to see some of them from the footpath. They are descended from those found on the island of Soay in the St Kilda archipelago. They are smaller than most domestic*

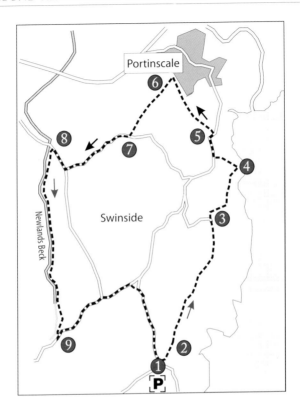

breeds and are self-shedding. No-one knows when the sheep arrived on Soay, but evidence suggests they came with the first human settlers around 4,000 years ago. When the Norsemen arrived at St Kilda in the 9th century, they named the island Sauda-ey – 'Island of Sheep'.

3. Cross straight over the Lingholm driveway and follow the path towards Portinscale. This quickly forks and you bear right along the wider of the two routes.

The gardens to the right belong to Lingholm and, although they are no longer open to the public, you will be able to see some of the rhododendron in the woodland fringing the path. The trees in this area are alive with the sound of birdsong – as well as a variety of tits and finches, you may catch sight of the occasional tree creeper and nuthatch.

Between 1885, when she was 19, and 1907, Beatrix Potter spent nine summer holidays at Lingholm, and it was here that she sketched the squirrels while working on The Tale Of Squirrel Nutkin. *The view of Cat Bells was also used in the book, and St Herbert's Island in Derwentwater is renamed Owl Island, the destination of a convoy of squirrels who cross the lake on rafts. Potter also spent one holiday at the Fawe Estate, closer to Nichol End. The gardens here are said to have formed the basis for the gardens in* The Tale Of Benjamin Bunny.

Although born in London, it was Potter's cherished memories of holidays in the Lakes that inspired her love of the countryside. As a young woman, she became friends with Canon Hardwicke Rawnsley, one of the co-founders of the National Trust, and his views on the need to protect the natural beauty of the area had a profound effect on the writer. She eventually moved to Cumbria and gained the respect of local people as a top breeder of Herdwick sheep, the Lake District's own, hardy breed. When she died in 1943, she left 14 Lakeland farms – a total of 4,000 acres – to the National Trust.

4. Cross straight over the next driveway – towards Nichol End and Portinscale. Bear left along the Nichol End Marine driveway and then turn right at the road.

5. Walk along the road for about 300 metres and then turn left along a surfaced lane with a footpath sign beside it. After another third of a mile, take the footpath on your left. The signpost is hard to spot – you

don't see it until you're standing just a few metres away.

6. The narrow, fenced path leads down to a small footbridge, beyond which you cross a field on a constructed path.

> *You are now heading towards the forested slopes of Swinside. The peaks to the right of this little hill are Causey Pike, Barrow and, across Coledale, Grisedale Pike.*

7. Pass to the left of Yew Tree Cottage along a narrow, fenced trail. Go through the gate at the top of the steps and then turn right along the road, passing the cottage and Ullock Farm. At the next T-junction, turn right and then, in approximately 250 metres, go through the small, signposted gate on your left, close to an old stone bridge.

8. You now walk along the gorse-fringed banks of Newlands Beck. A few metres after passing a humpback bridge over the beck, you reach a gate where you have to head back on to the top of the embankment via a wooden stile to the right.

9. When you finally reach the road, turn left. Beyond the Swinside Inn at the top of the hill, carefully follow the road round to the right and then take the next road turning on your right (towards Grange). Turn right again at the T-junction. Ignoring a turning on your left to the Hawse End centre, you eventually return to the road bend at the base of Cat Bells. Cross the cattle grid and, where the road bends sharp left, turn right to retrace your steps to the car park.

2

RIVER DERWENT
& THE BASE OF CASTLE CRAG

This is a low-level walk consisting of two contrasting halves. The first half passes through pleasant valley woodland and beside the River Derwent; the second half crosses open fellside above Borrowdale. Although only a few hundred feet of height is gained, the views on the return route are lovely. The paths can be a little rough in places, but they are generally easy to follow. The only difficulty comes early in the walk when a slab of exposed rock at the river's edge has to be negotiated.

Start/Finish: Seatoller National Trust car park (NY245138)
Distance: 7.6km (4.7 miles)
Height gain: 251m (823ft)

1. From the far corner of the car park, walk up the broad track and through the gate at the top. Bear right and then stay on the level, right-hand path at the fork. Going through a small gate in the wall on the right, you begin a pleasant stroll through pretty mixed woodland.

> *If you are lucky, you may hear the sound of the Borrowdale cuckoo. Legend has it that the good people of this valley once built a wall across their beautiful dale to keep the cuckoo in so that spring would last forever. When the bird inevitably flew over the barricade, one of the dalesmen cried: "By gow! If we'd nobbut laid another line o' stanes atop, we'd a copped 'im!" This is supposedly why the dialect word for cuckoo – "gowk" – also means "fool".*

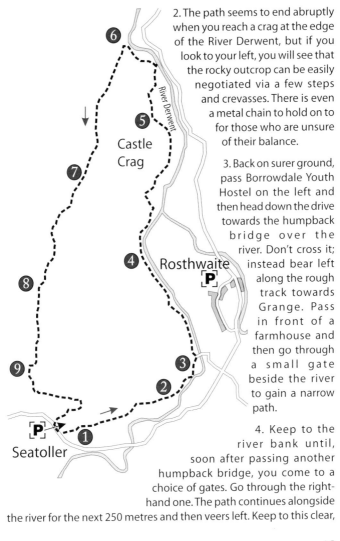

2. The path seems to end abruptly when you reach a crag at the edge of the River Derwent, but if you look to your left, you will see that the rocky outcrop can be easily negotiated via a few steps and crevasses. There is even a metal chain to hold on to for those who are unsure of their balance.

3. Back on surer ground, pass Borrowdale Youth Hostel on the left and then head down the drive towards the humpback bridge over the river. Don't cross it; instead bear left along the rough track towards Grange. Pass in front of a farmhouse and then go through a small gate beside the river to gain a narrow path.

4. Keep to the river bank until, soon after passing another humpback bridge, you come to a choice of gates. Go through the right-hand one. The path continues alongside the river for the next 250 metres and then veers left. Keep to this clear,

13

wide track as it meanders through the woods at the base of Castle Crag.

You are currently on part of the Cumbria Way, one of two long-distance routes encountered on this walk. This popular, 70-mile path runs from Ulverston in the south of the county to the historic city of Carlisle in the north via Coniston, Langdale, Borrowdale, Derwentwater and the Northern Fells. Later in the walk, as you traverse the fellside above Borrowdale, you follow in the footsteps of long-distance hikers on the Allerdale Ramble. This 54-mile route starts in Borrowdale and then heads up towards Skiddaw before reaching the coast on the Solway Firth and joining the Cumbria Coastal Way as far as Grune Point.

5. Having passed some quarry workings and a spoil heap, bear right at a clear fork to head uphill along the wider of the paths. At the next junction, turn right, still following signposts for Grange. Don't be tempted by any minor paths off this clear route as you lose what little height you've gained and rejoin the River Derwent.

6. Turn left at a footpath sign just above a bridge over a tributary beck. This is signposted Seatoller and Honister. The climb is fairly gentle as you leave the woods via a gate, but it's a slow plod up the stony bridleway beyond.

Castle Crag up to your left is crowned by the remains of an Iron Age hill fort. The Romans also used it, taking advantage of its prominent, strategic position within the valley. But the crag has been occupied more recently than that. Between the two world wars, two of the crag's caves became the summer home of Millican Dalton.

Dalton was born in Alston, Cumberland in 1867, but his parents moved to Essex when he was young. Sick of being a commuter in southern England, he left a comfortable career in the City when he was in his 30s to offer adventure holidays to would-be climbers in the Lake District.

Desperate to get back to nature, Dalton lived at first in a tent, then in a split-level quarried cave half way up Castle Crag. Despite having a waterfall pouring through his roof, he turned one cave into a living area and one into a bedroom, which he called "The Attic".

Intelligent and well-educated, Dalton loved to pit himself against the elements. He climbed trees in winter to keep fit for climbing and, on his 50th ascent of Napes Needle, lit a fire on the tiny summit and made a pot of coffee. A dump in the nearby village of Grange helped him make ends meet – by providing basics such as old pans and materials he could make into camping equipment for sale to his climbing customers.

During the London Blitz on 1940/41, he braved snow, ice and sub-zero temperatures to remain all winter on Castle Crag. Sadly, he didn't get to end his days on his beloved fells; he died in hospital in Amersham after contracting pneumonia in 1947 – at the age of 79.

7. At the top of the low pass, you are rewarded with views of Borrowdale and its surrounding fells. About 150 metres beyond the pass, turn left at a cairn near a small waymarker – along a narrower path heading briefly downhill.

8. Contouring the grassy fellside above Borrowdale, you cross several streams and go through several gates, only reluctantly abandoning this easy path when you reach two gates next to each other. Choose the left-hand one (towards Seatoller) and head down the grassy slope in a SE direction, turning left when you reach a broad track.

9. It is possible to cut a corner here, but older knees may prefer to keep to the track – it descends in a rather roundabout fashion, but the gradient is much easier. Turn left at the road and the car park is on the left just after the last building in Seatoller.

3

BASE OF CAT BELLS & DERWENTWATER SHORE

A boat trip across Derwentwater on the Keswick Launch is followed by a mostly easy walk – with just one or two gentle climbs – along a bridleway tucked away at the base of Cat Bells and Maiden Moor. The outward route goes as far as Grange and then returns via the lakeshore. Aside from a short stretch from Manesty to Grange, the paths are good underfoot.

Both halves of the walk are endowed with some wonderful views, and the chances are that, if you are here mid-week, you will have the terrace path to yourself.

Start/Finish: Hawes End jetty on Derwentwater (NY251213)
Distance: 9.5km (5.9 miles)
Height gain: 267m (875ft)

---

1. Get off the boat at Hawes End. Follow the line of the fence up to and through a kissing-gate, beyond which a clear path leads up to the Hawes End centre access road. Turn right and then left to climb alongside a drystone wall – towards Cat Bells and the Newlands Valley.

2. Turn left at the road and then go through the pedestrian gate to the left of the cattle grid. Follow the clear path alongside a fence up to the road. Cross over and head a little to the left to pick up a clear, wide bridleway going gently uphill.

This lovely terrace path skirts the lower slopes of Cat Bells and, later, Maiden Moor, never climbing above 200m, but always providing great views of the lake and Borrowdale.

There are lots of benches along the route, one of which is dedicated to writer Sir Hugh Walpole. It overlooks his former home, Brackenburn.

Hugh Walpole was born in New Zealand in 1884 and lived in Cumbria from 1924 until his death in 1941. Brackenburn, his "little paradise on Cat Bells", was originally a bungalow built of Honister slate in 1909. He enlarged it and converted the upper story of the nearby garage into a study, which eventually housed his library of 30,000 books and his collection of paintings. Literary visitors to the house included JB Priestley, Arthur Ransome and WH Auden.

Walpole wrote a great deal while at Brackenburn, including his Cumberland family saga The Herries Chronicle.

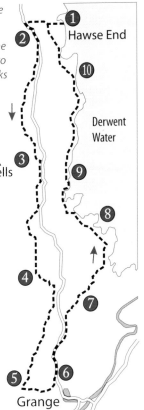

3. At one point, the bridleway descends to the road, but it then continues immediately after a small parking area. Almost a mile-and-a-half after joining the bridleway, the route divides at a drystone wall bordering an area of woodland. Keep left here (gently downhill) with the wall on your immediate left.

4. You join a wide path that drops down to a gate. Do not go through

17

the gate; instead turn right along the permitted path – towards Hollows Farm and Seatoller – walking initially with the fence close by on your left.

> *Looking up to Black Crag to the right here, you may be able to make out some of the scars left by the many mines that once operated in this area. There are several trials here and one or two adits.*

> *A little further on and the remains of some of the earliest German workings in the area, dating back to about 1566, can be seen above Grange. This is part of the Copperplate Copper Mine. The ore would have been ferried across Derwentwater and then carted to the smelter at Brigham, Keswick.*

5. The narrow path, which soon becomes considerably rougher, eventually crosses a wooden footbridge followed by a step stile. Beyond this, follow the line of the wall on your left down the slope and through a gate in the wall corner. A narrow path now leads down to the road.

> *The gathering of slate buildings a few hundred metres to the right belong to the tiny village of Grange-in-Borrowdale. This was originally a large sheep farm – or 'grange' – run by the Cistercian monks of Furness Abbey.*

6. Turn left along the road for just over half a kilometre and then turn right through a gate and along a clear track – signposted Lodore.

> *About 100 metres to the left of the path, there is an ancient salt well which was credited in the 18th century with curative powers. The monks of Furness Abbey are believed to have extracted salt here.*

> *Again, there are mine workings dotted all over the place here and, if you know what you're looking for, they are reasonably easy to spot – a heap of treated copper not far off the path comes from the old Manesty copper workings; there are 16th century chippings in the exposed bedrock at the lake's edge; and close to the shore is a flooded shaft*

dating from around 1580.

7. After going through two kissing-gates, the path divides. Bear left here. At the next fork, immediately after crossing a boggy stretch via a short section of boardwalk, bear right towards the lake. On reaching a T-junction a few metres back from the water's edge, turn left.

8. Follow the popular, constructed track until you reach a rough lane at a slate bungalow called The Warren. Turn right here. Soon after the next gate, bear right at a fork in the path, staying close to the water's edge.

The spoil heaps in this area are the remains of a large and productive lead mine which was worked from the end of the 17th century until 1891. Miners worked below the level of the lake bed and the site was plagued by water ingress from subteranean springs. A steam engine was eventually used to pump the water out, but this was an expensive undertaking. Just above the lake are the remains of the engine house. The nearby cottage was the manager's house.

9. On entering the woods, choose the lakeside path.

This is Brandlehow Park, the National Trust's first Lake District acquisition. It was bought by public subscription in 1902 to prevent housing development. Princess Louise, Queen Victoria's daughter, presided over the official opening. After the ceremony, she and the three National Trust founders – Canon Hardwicke Rawnsley, Robert Hunter and Octavia Hill – each planted an oak tree.

10. As you leave the woods via a gate, you are faced with a choice of two wide tracks. Take the one on the left and follow it up to a metalled road. Turn right here, passing below the Hawes End outdoor centre, and then turn right again to descend a signposted trail to the Hawes End jetty.

4

WALLA CRAG & ASHNESS BRIDGE

Walla Crag (379m) is one of Borrowdale's best viewpoints – with unrivalled views of Derwentwater and across to Skiddaw. This walk uses a good path across the open fellside to reach the top of the crag and then returns via the ancient forest of Great Wood. The climbs are relatively gentle and well spaced-out.

Start/Finish: Ashness Bridge car park (NY269196)
Distance: 6.7km (4.2 miles)
Height gain: 346m (1,134ft)

---

1. Turn left along the road and cross Ashness Bridge. Almost immediately, turn sharp right – not along the signposted path, but up the less distinct one heading SE. Crossing a stile, you continue uphill in the same direction until you reach a junction of paths just to the left of a footbridge over Barrow Beck. Turn left along this clear track and go through the next gate.

2. Derwentwater is far below now as you climb at a relatively easy angle across the open fell towards Walla Crag. Reaching a stile in a wall, cross it for the final pull to the top of the crag.

> *The views from the summit are amazing. Looking from the left, you can see up into Borrowdale, Derwentwater below, Bassenthwaite Lake (beyond that is Criffel in Dumfries & Galloway), Skiddaw and Blencathra.*
>
> *There are several islands in Derwentwater, and each of them has an interesting history. Derwent Isle, the most northerly, was once home to a group of German miners*

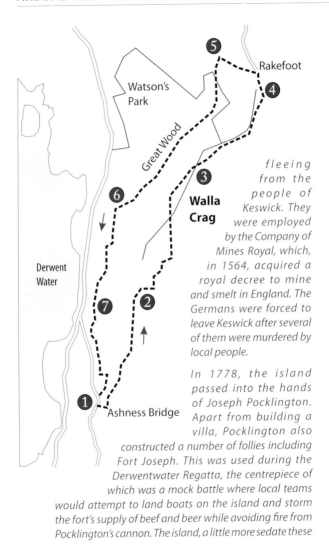

fleeing from the people of Keswick. They were employed by the Company of Mines Royal, which, in 1564, acquired a royal decree to mine and smelt in England. The Germans were forced to leave Keswick after several of them were murdered by local people.

In 1778, the island passed into the hands of Joseph Pocklington. Apart from building a villa, Pocklington also constructed a number of follies including Fort Joseph. This was used during the Derwentwater Regatta, the centrepiece of which was a mock battle where local teams would attempt to land boats on the island and storm the fort's supply of beef and beer while avoiding fire from Pocklington's cannon. The island, a little more sedate these *days, is now owned by the National Trust.*

The most central of the islands is St Herbert's Isle, named after a religious recluse who lived here in the 7th century. He was the long-time friend and disciple of St Cuthbert, Bishop of Lindisfarne. A chapel was consecrated on the island when the cult of St Herbert was revived in 1374.

3. Head away from the top in a NE direction to follow a path that skirts the edge of the crag and then drops to a kissing-gate. Go through and turn left along a wide, grassy path. With a wall on your left, you plunge down into the valley that hides Brockle Beck and through a gate to gain access to a clear track.

4. Drop down to a narrow bridge. Crossing the beck here, turn left along the surfaced lane for 200 metres and then left again along a footpath - signposted Keswick and Great Wood. Recross Brockle Beck via another narrow footbridge and then turn right, heading downstream.

5. About 300 metres beyond this bridge – and just above a radio mast – turn left towards Great Wood and Borrowdale. The narrow path soon leads into the woods and joins a wider track coming in from the right.

6. Continue in the same direction and, after almost a mile, turn left at a T-junction. When the path splits – just after reaching a paved section – bear right to cross Cat Gill via a narrow footbridge. The clear path now heads downhill with a wall on the right for a while before swinging left across more open ground at the foot of Falcon Crag.

At the top of Cat Gill, close to the summit of Walla Crag, is a steep gully called Lady's Rake. This is reputedly the route by which Lady Derwentwater fled from Lord's Island in 1715 on hearing of the impending execution of her husband for his role in the Jacobite uprising of that year. The Highlanders, proclaiming James Stuart as king, under the title of James III, got as far as Preston, where they surrendered to General Willis. James Radcliffe, the third and last Earl of Derwentwater, was one of the many members of prominent local families who had adhered to the old faith and supported the Jacobites. Although he pleaded guilty when he appeared before the privy council on January 10, 1716, and begged for mercy, blaming his participation in the uprising on youth and inexperience, he was executed on Tower Hill and his lands confiscated by the Crown.

7. When you reach a cairn and signpost marking a fork, take the higher, left-hand route, climbing very gradually towards Ashness Bridge. Having gone through a gate in a drystone wall, drop down to the road and turn left to retrace your steps to the car park.

Just below Ashness Bridge, close to the shores of Derwentwater, is Barrow House, which has been a youth hostel since 1961. It was built in the 1780s by Joseph Pocklington, the Derwent Isle eccentric.

In the 1930s, Barrow House was run as a guest house by Bob Graham, the originator of the Bob Graham Round. This 72-mile route, still one of Lakeland's most serious challenges, was first completed by Graham in 1932. Originally from near Carlisle, it took him just 23 hours and 39 minutes to scale the 42 peaks involved, climbing about 27,000ft in the process. His record was to stand for 28 years. To date, about 1,200 people have managed to complete the round in less than 24 hours. The record is now held by Billy Bland, who, in 1982, managed it in 13 hours and 53 minutes.

5

LATRIGG & THE RAILWAY PATH

Latrigg (368m) is a grassy little hill that crouches at the base of mighty Skiddaw. Aside from a bit of mud after wet weather, you are unlikely to experience any difficulties on this walk – it's a pleasant stroll on good paths with just one short climb; and there are great views of Derwentwater and the surrounding fells from the top. The return route is along the disused Cockermouth, Keswick and Penrith Railway, so it's almost completely flat.

Start/Finish: Spooney Green Lane (NY267241)
on the northern side of Keswick, just off Brundholme Road
If driving to the start, please park considerately
as this is a residential area
Distance: 9km (5.6 miles)
Height gain: 358m (1,174ft)

1. Spoony Green Lane is a wide lane heading NE from the Briar Rigg area of Keswick. The start of the lane is marked by a fingerpost, which reads: "Public Bridleway Skiddaw 4 miles." Head up the lane and cross the bridge over the busy A66.

2. Having passed through a gate near Spooney Green B&B, you start making your way uphill on a wide track. Soon after joining another track coming in from the right, the route crosses a tiny beck as it swings left. Ignoring a shortcut on the right, you then swing right with the main track to reach a fork. Bear left here.

The mixed woodlands of Latrigg contain a rich variety of birdlife, as well as red squirrels, roe deer and badgers. As in many parts of Cumbria, foresters are encouraging natural regrowth of oak, ash, birch, hazel and other native species. Many non-native conifers are being felled, although some are allowed to remain because the red squirrels love the cones.

3. The climb eases considerably and you soon find yourself walking with a fenced plantation on your left. When the trees begin to thin out, turn sharp right – almost heading back on yourself – to climb the northern slopes of Latrigg on a clear, zigzagging path. Eventually, the zig-zags end and you join up with the wheelchair route coming up from the left.

4. Follow this mostly level path as it curves round the gully to a bench. This is a great spot to rest and admire the fantastic views – over Keswick and Derwentwater and across to the fells of the Coledale and Robinson rounds – before swinging left for the last, easy bit of the climb.

5. The summit of Latrigg isn't marked. You only realise you've reached it when the path ahead starts to drop. Keep to this clear path along the southern edge of the fell and through a gate in a fence, beyond which it becomes grassier and a little more indistinct.

6. Having walked about three-quarters of a mile from the bench, the path appears to make straight for a fence. Bear left here, still with a faint path on

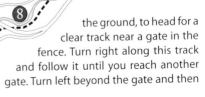

the ground, to head for a clear track near a gate in the fence. Turn right along this track and follow it until you reach another gate. Turn left beyond the gate and then immediately right down a surfaced lane.

7. As you approach the River Greta, watch for a gate to your right – signposted Keswick and Threlkeld. Go through this and then through another gate providing access to the railway footpath close to a small shelter. Once on the old railway, turn right. It's hard to go wrong now – this clear, wide, level track takes you all the way back to Keswick.

This track is part of the 50km Cockermouth, Keswick and Penrith Railway, built by Thomas Bouch in 1865. It brought coke from the Durham coal mines to the iron-making industry on the west coast. Improvements in the making of coke from West Cumberland coal saw this traffic decline quickly after 1910. The western end of the line, together with the link from Cockermouth to Workington, was closed in 1966. The remaining section closed in 1972.

There is plenty of interest as you walk the old track, crossing and recrossing the River Greta via several bridges. The river has been used for industrial purposes for more than six centuries. In the early 19th century, it provided power for a pencil mill, several bobbin mills and a textile mill. You pass the site of one old mill near Low Briery. This was known locally as the "Fancy Bottoms Mill" because it made the intricate edgings for waistcoats. It closed in 1961. By the mid-19th century, there were 120 water-powered bobbin mills in the Lake District. They produced about half of the entire world textile industry's bobbins.

8. Soon after passing Low Briery and its caravan site, you reach a section of boardwalk as the track, temporarily abandoning the line of the railway, negotiates the increasingly steep-sided gorge. It then goes under the massive A66 road bridge.

This hideous monstrosity won the surprising accolade of Best Concrete Engineering Structure of the Century in 1999.

9. Having passed through the Brigham area of Keswick and crossed

the river one last time, the track ends at the platform buildings of the old Keswick Station, now owned by the Keswick Country House Hotel. Keep straight ahead and when you reach the leisure centre's service road, turn right.

The Brigham area of Keswick was once a noisy, smelly hub of furnaces, smelting houses and stamp mills processing the ore extracted by the men of the Company of Mines Royal from the surrounding fells and dales. By 1567, there were at least six furnaces operating in the area. Dozens of men were employed to cart peat from Skiddaw Forest, Wythop Moss and the Helvellyn range to use as fuel, and dales were stripped of woodland to create charcoal.

10. You need to bear left at the small roundabout – along Brundholme Road – but don't head off yet; look to the right of the roundabout, on the other side of the road, and you will see a small footpath at the top of a few steps. This path provides a safer, more pleasant alternative to the road. It crosses straight over one minor road and then ends as you reach the houses at Briar Rigg. Continue along the road in the same direction and you will soon see Spoony Green Lane, the place where the walk started, on your right.

The first settlement at Keswick was at Great Crosthwaite. The church here was built in 553AD and named after St Kentigern (also known as St Mungo), the 6th century bishop of Glasgow. Having been persecuted for his views, he fled Scotland to preach in Wales. On his journey south, he stopped in Carlisle where he discovered that the local people were "given to idolatry". He decided on a short stay in the region to try to educate them. He set up a cross at Great Crosthwaite, which gave rise to the name 'Crosfeld', meaning 'cross in the clearing'.

6

DODD

In 2002, the Forestry Commission felled the trees from the top of Dodd (502m), leaving walkers with some great views to the north, west and south. To the east, the views are blocked by the Skiddaw massif, on which little Dodd is nothing more than an insignificant pimple.

This short walk climbs quickly – and fairly steeply -to the summit via forest tracks and waymarked paths. It then drops back down the western side of the fell along a less well-used, but lovely path with good views over Bassenthwaite Lake, and a chance of seeing the ospreys that nest nearby.

Start/Finish: Dodd Wood car park
near Mirehouse (NY235281)
Distance: 4.8km (3 miles)
Height gain: 393m (1,290ft)

---

1. Cross the footbridge behind the Old Sawmill Tearoom and then walk uphill along the clear track until you reach a surfaced forest lane. Turn right to begin a reasonably steep climb alongside Skill Beck, which is in the steep-sided ravine to the right.

2. Eventually the trees thin out and you join one track coming in from the left, soon followed by another coming in from the right. Almost immediately after the second junction, turn right along a narrower track heading uphill, signposted Dodd summit.

3. Almost immediately, the track swings right and you are met by a wonderful view towards Derwentwater and the fells surrounding it, an uplifting contrast to the confines of the forest. There's also a handy

bench from which to enjoy the sight.

4. Climbing more gently, you pass a narrow, green way-marked trail off to the left. This marks the start of your return route later, but for now keep to the main path as it swings sharp right. It quickly winds its way to the summit, which is marked by a tall memorial stone.

In the 1860s, Dodd was home to a Scottish hermit called George Smith. He lived in a wigwam on a ledge on the fell, staying there in all weathers because he loved being close to nature.

H i s shelter consisted of a low stone wall and a framework of branches and reeds as a roof. Known as the Skiddaw Hermit, he made ends meet by painting farmers and their wives, although his favourite subjects were said to be local pub landlords who paid his fees in whisky. He

29

also did character assessments at local fairs by feeling the shape of people's heads. George's weakness for alcohol got him into trouble with the police on several occasions and he eventually returned to Scotland, where he died in a psychiatric home.

5. When you can tear yourself away from the view, retrace your steps as far as the green way-marked trail. Turn right here and, in a few metres, turn right again to head downhill. As you descend, you will cross straight over a grassy, disused forest track – simply keep following the green waymarkers.

6. The path re-enters the trees before traversing the fellside high above Bassenthwaite Lake. This is a lovely stretch of walking – you can really stride out as you take in the views. The path then drops to a wide track, along which you turn right.

7. Turn left at the next track junction and then take the first turning on the right.

Dodd Wood is famously home to a pair of ospreys, and special viewing platforms with high-powered telescopes have been set up. The Forestry Commission and National Park authority spent years trying to encourage these fish-eating birds of prey back to Cumbria after they were persecuted to extinction in the UK by the early part of the 20th century. They built tree-top platforms for the birds, and, finally, in 2001, a passing pair took a fancy to one of these and decided to set up home. The birds spend the summer here and then return to Africa in the winter.

8. Turn right at a crossing of paths. Walking alongside Skill Beck again, you soon drop back down into the car park near the tearoom.

Just across the road from the car park is Mirehouse. This elegant house, close to the shores of Bassenthwaite Lake, was built in 1666. Many famous writers, including Wordsworth, Tennyson, Southey and Thomas Carlyle, were entertained here.

7

BARROW

You can't miss Barrow (455m) as you drive along the A66 from Keswick towards Braithwaite. The clear route following its shapely north-east ridge is just crying out to be walked. This is one of the hardest walks in this book – not in terms of total height gained and definitely not in terms of distance, but simply because almost all of the climbing is done in one go. Having said that, Barrow is one of the best low-level ridges in the entire Lake District, with steep ground tumbling away on either side of a broad, mostly grassy ridge path – it's well worth the effort.

Start/Finish: Parking area to the west of the
Methodist chapel in Braithwaite (NY229236)
Distance: 5km (3.1 miles)
Height gain: 375m (1,232ft)

---

1. Standing on the asphalt lane with your back to the white-washed Methodist chapel, turn left and head towards the centre of the village. In just a few strides, take the rough vehicle track on your right, soon walking with Coledale Beck on your left.

2. At the road junction, ignore the sharp turn on the right – that's just a dead-end – instead, turn right along the road towards Newlands. In a few more metres, turn right up a track towards Braithwaite Lodge. On approaching the farm, the path heads to the right of the main buildings. As you pass a small out-building on your right, head for the large wooden gate straight ahead and cross the stile immediately to the right of it – signposted Newlands. With a fence on your right, climb easily to a small gate in the field corner and, once through, swing left on the clear path.

3. When you reach a junction of paths marked by a squat fingerpost, turn right to begin the climb up Barrow's mostly grassy north-east ridge. The superb views from the top – up Coledale and across to Causey Pike – are a fair reward for the effort.

> It is hard to imagine it now, but peaceful Coledale was once home to a thriving mining industry. Force Crag Mine is a lead, zinc and baryte mine that has been worked intermittently since Elizabethan times. A lead vein was first located at Coledale Head in 1578, although concentrated mining didn't start until the early part of the 19th century. The last attempt to extract ore was made by the New Coledale Mining Company in 1984, but the firm left in 1990 after a large collapse flooded part of the workings. The mine was declared a Scheduled Ancient Monument in 2003 and public safety work was carried out on the buildings. The National Trust now runs occasional tours of the site.
>
> There is also evidence of mining on Barrow and in nearby Stonycroft Gill, where lead was extracted from about 1680 to 1854. Stonycroft Gill was the scene of an early mining tragedy. A shaft had been sunk into the stream bed and the beck diverted via a dam. After a period of exceptionally heavy rain, the dam burst and the beck reverted to its original course, flooding the workings and drowning several miners. The men's remains weren't recovered until several years later.

4. Dropping away from the summit, the ridge route heads WSW to arrive at Barrow Door, the pass between Barrow and Stile End. The path splits on the way down. Choose either option.

5. From the pass, turn right (NNE). As you descend, don't be tempted by the path off to the right, heading down towards the beck; keep heading in the general direction of Skiddaw in the distance. Passing the ruins of High Coledale, partially hidden by trees on your left, you join up with

a track. Continue in the same direction, through a gate and then along a lane on the edge of Braithwaite.

6. When you draw level with the Coledale Inn on your left, turn right – not along the signposted footpath, but down a rough track. This leads back to the chapel.

The famous Cumberland Pencil Company, established in the mid-19th century, was originally located in Braithwaite. The Coledale Inn, once used as a woollen mill, was then the private home of the factory manager. The company moved to Keswick in 1898 after the Braithwaite factory was destroyed by fire. It has since moved to west Cumbria, although the museum remains in Keswick.

Local legend has it that in the early 1500s, a violent storm in Borrowdale led to trees being uprooted and the discovery of an unknown black material underneath. Shepherds then began using the mysterious substance to mark their sheep, creating the world's first pencils. The material, of course, turned out to be graphite, known locally as 'wad'.

8

HIGH RIGG, ST JOHN'S IN THE VALE

Although the summit of High Rigg is only 357m above sea level, its short, undulating ridge provides a wonderful walk amid beautiful mountain scenery – a sort of Lake District in miniature. In fact, this is a great route for introducing young people to fell-walking. The hard work is over early in the walk with a brief, but quite steep, grassy climb up to the summit cairn. The ridge path is generally easy to follow – although it does become a little boggy in one place - and the return route follows the pretty valley of St John's Beck through woodland and beside farmland.

Start/Finish: St John's Church,
about 3km south of Threlkeld (NY306225)
Distance: 8km (5 miles)
Height gain: 375m (1,230ft)

---

1. With your back to the church, turn left along the lane. Immediately after the diocesan youth centre, turn left to follow the narrow path around the back of the building to a kissing-gate in the wall.

2. Go through the gate and head straight up the northern ridge of High Rigg – a short, but sharp climb. As you approach the highest point, the grassy path becomes wider and more track-like. It swings right to pass in front of a crag that is home to the summit cairn. Once you've visited the cairn, return to the track – it soon swings left to winds its way, in a generally southerly direction, across the knobbly top to the corner of a drystone wall.

3. Having reached the wall, walk gently uphill with it on your left and then aim to the right of some soggy ground in a depression straight

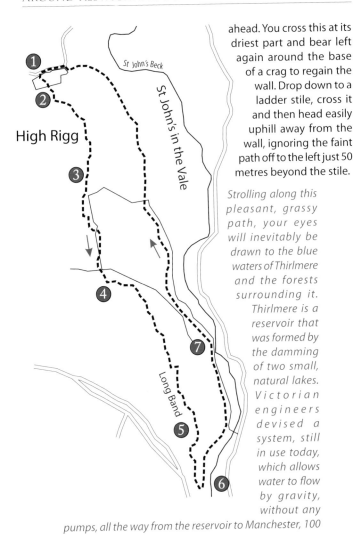

ahead. You cross this at its driest part and bear left again around the base of a crag to regain the wall. Drop down to a ladder stile, cross it and then head easily uphill away from the wall, ignoring the faint path off to the left just 50 metres beyond the stile.

Strolling along this pleasant, grassy path, your eyes will inevitably be drawn to the blue waters of Thirlmere and the forests surrounding it. Thirlmere is a reservoir that was formed by the damming of two small, natural lakes. Victorian engineers devised a system, still in use today, which allows water to flow by gravity, without any pumps, all the way from the reservoir to Manchester, 100 miles away. The water flows at a speed of about 6km per hour and takes just over a day to reach the city.

It was in 1874 that Manchester Corporation advisers realised that the city's ever increasing demand for water, then averaging 18 million gallons per day, would soon exhaust the supply. They first recommended sourcing water from Ullswater, but it was later decided to create Thirlmere. Despite being stalled by the Thirlmere Defence Association, the project eventually received Royal Assent in 1879 and Manchester was granted the right to extract 25 gallons of water per head per day. The first water to arrive in Manchester from Thirlmere was marked with an official ceremony on October 13, 1894.

4. Keeping to the path as it swings round to the left, you cross a stile in a wire fence and soon find yourself on a more open ridge, known as Long Band. This ends suddenly as you veer left to drop down a steep, loose path to a gap in a wall. *The path is badly eroded here, so watch your footing on the descent.*

5. Beyond the gap, there is one more short section of climbing before the path starts dropping away down the fell's southern ridge.

As you head down through the Scots pines, you will catch glimpses of a large, bare rockface across the valley to your left. This is Castle Rock, so-named because 18th century travellers on their way from Ambleside to Keswick used to see it and believe it was a castle. On approaching it, however, it turned into a simple crag. This was explained locally as being the work of the castle's guardian genie who wanted to keep strangers away.

Sir Walter Scott made the vale of St John the main setting for his Bride of Triermain. *It is at Castle Rock that Sir Walter has King Arthur dallying with the fortress's fairy inhabitants while on his way to Carlisle.*

6. Having reached a T-junction of paths just above the main road, turn left to walk along a narrow path around the side of the fell. There is a steep drop on the right down to St John's Beck at first, but you soon reach the valley floor and, a little later on, Low Bridge End Farm – a friendly spot to stop for a warming drink and a slice of cake.

7. The valley path continues to the left of a wall and through pleasant woodland before opening out to allow Blencathra to fill the vista ahead. Cruelly, the last part of the walk is an uphill trudge, albeit at relatively easy angle, but it's not what you want at this point in the walk. Don't despair though – you eventually reach the road. When you do, turn left to return to the church.

The name St John's in the Vale is derived from the Knights Hospitaller of the Order of St John of Jerusalem, who are thought to have had a hospice or church here in the 13th century. The knights, also known as the Knights of Rhodes or the Knights of Malta, were a Christian organisation established in Jerusalem in 1080 to care for sick or injured pilgrims to the Holy Land. After the First Crusade in 1099, they became a religious and military order charged with defending the Holy Land.

Today's church of St John's was built in 1845 and the quiet lane here was once an important route to Keswick from Matterdale. The churchyard contains the grave of John Richardson, a dialect poet. Born in 1817, he was initially a builder and helped in the building of the church, the school next door in 1849 and the vicarage in 1856. Later, he became a teacher and then a poet. His first book, Cummerland Talk, *was published in 1871, just 15 years before he died.*

9

Barf & Lord's Seat

Starting from the Whinlatter Visitor Centre, located at just over 300m above sea level, you get a significant head-start on your climb up to Barf (463m) and then on to Lord's Seat (552m). If you're hoping to see some of the surrounding countryside, don't let the fact that most of the walk is spent on Forestry Commission land put you off – there are only a few places where the views are blocked by trees. In fact, the sudden appearance of the massive bulk of Skiddaw or the shapely Grisedale Pike through a gap in the conifers adds to the appeal of this walk. Navigation is aided by forestry waymarkers and the use of good, solid tracks. The paths on the open fell are clear on the ground, but can get a bit boggy between Barf and Lord's Seat.

Start/Finish: Whinlatter Visitor Centre (NY207244)
Distance: 7.6km (4.7 miles)
Height gain: 416m (1,363ft)

---

1. From the parking area, walk ENE along the asphalt track, passing directly in front of the visitor centre, which is to your left. You soon reach a fork, marked by a numbered post (15), where you bear right to pass a white cottage on your right.

> *The views ahead towards Skiddaw briefly open out as you approach a sharp left-hand bend at post number 14. Ignore the track off to the right here as you follow the wide forest road up into thicker forest.*

2. The track swings right twice, and you must leave it on the second occasion. You'll see a faint path to the left as you approach this sweeping

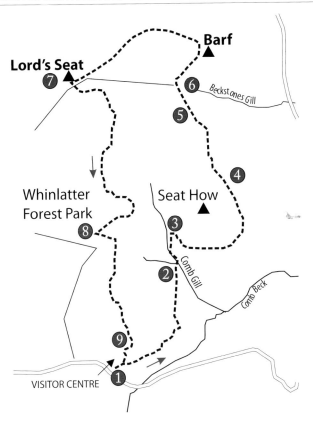

bend. Ignore this; instead, wait until the track has crossed the beck and then turn left along a narrow, gravel path, the start of which is marked by a red-topped post. You climb steeply at first – with the beck on your left.

3. At the top of the climb, turn right along the wider track. At the next T-junction, turn right again – along an even broader track. This heads briefly downhill until it hits a fork at post number nine. Bear left here, heading uphill.

4. When you reach the next fork (at post number eight), bear right to join a descending track.

> With craggy slopes dropping away steeply on the right, you can see Thornthwaite far below and a distinctive white rock on the lower slopes of Barf. This is known as Bishop Rock or the Bishop of Barf. In 1783, while staying at a hotel in Thornthwaite, the Bishop of Derry, a little the worse for drink, had a wager with the locals that he could ride over Barf to Whitehaven. The next day, he and his horse headed up the steep, scree-covered fell. His wager - and his life - came to a sudden end when he slipped and plunged down the fellside. The white rock marks the spot at which he fell, and it is still painted regularly by staff at a local hotel.

5. Having passed – and ignored – a right-turn down through the trees at post number 21, climb to a fork. Bear right here, along a narrow path that leads to the forest boundary fence.

6. Cross the stile and drop down to Beckstones Gill, which is easily forded. From here, the clear path climbs steadily on the open fell to the summit of Barf. From Barf your next target is Lord's Seat, the small top to the WSW. The path between the two is clear. It leaves Barf's summit in a WNW direction, soon veering west, and winds between several little knolls and across some boggy ground.

> Like many place names in Cumbria, the origins of Barf lie in the old Norse language. The fell was formerly known as Barrugh Fell, which is said to be derived from the old Norse 'berg' meaning 'mountain'. Barrugh, which is also a local surname, is correctly pronounced Barf.

7. From the top, descend the well-trodden path towards the stile that takes you back within the forest's boundary. Follow the surfaced path on the other side, and then bear right at a fork.

> The Whinlatter forests cover more than 10 square miles. The Forestry Commission's first planting in the Lake

*District was at Hospital Plantation, close to the head of
Whinlatter Pass, in 1919. The area got its name because
it used to be the site of a "fever hospital". Fever hospitals
were established in the second half of the 19th century to
treat infectious diseases such as typhus, diphtheria and
scarlet fever.*

8. You will reach a T-junction of forestry tracks at a clear, open area.
A sign to your left indicates this is Tarbarrel Moss. Turn left on to the
wide forestry road. This descends to another open area with a bench
and a choice of routes. Take the narrow path to the left of the bench.
Almost immediately it splits. Take the right-hand branch to head steeply
downhill.

9. In the final few hundred metres of the walk, you follow a twisting
route through the trees – turn right at the first junction; left at the
second one; and then right at the third one. Bear left at the next fork
and the path quickly drops you behind the visitor centre.

10

GRANGE FELL & WATENDLATH

If you expect all the fells above Borrowdale to be heaving with walkers, think again! King's How (392m) and Jopplety How (400m) are peaceful, heather-clad tops that are well off-the-beaten-track. The climb up from the valley is a steep one and this, along with the rugged nature of some of the paths, is what makes this the most difficult and adventurous walk in this book. But the rewards are numerous.

Start/Finish: Parking area on the B5289 Borrowdale road,
400 metres north of Grange (NY256176)
Distance: 8km (5 miles)
Height gain: 448m (1,468ft)

---

1. Turn right along the road, heading in the general direction of Keswick, and then turn right along the first track you come to. Having gone through a gate near two cottages, the track approaches a beck and then suddenly ends. As it does so, veer right along a grassy path heading upstream. In about 200 metres, the path forks – bear right here to head gently uphill.

2. Cross a wooden step stile just above a small waterfall and then turn left along a clearer, pitched path. This is a steep path, but, because of the mossy, slippery nature of the rocks, it is better to use this route for the ascent rather than the descent.

3. As you emerge from the woods and cross a flat area, ignore the stile straight ahead and continue uphill along a clear path to the right of a fence. The path climbs to Long Moss where it swings right to avoid the damp ground, and then becomes a mess of large stones and muddy

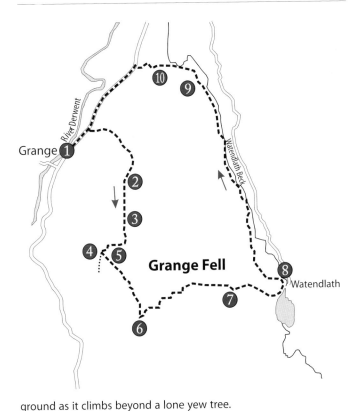

ground as it climbs beyond a lone yew tree.

It winds its way through the trees and on to the north-western side of King's How. Don't be tempted by a faint path to the right near a wall; you need to head up the exposed rocks to the left here. You may need your hands as you clamber upwards, but it's a short-lived scramble.

4. The path swings right near a cairn and soon passes a memorial plaque to King Edward VII before the final pull to the top.

Borrowdale is now revealed in all its glory ahead of you,

43

but if you turn around, the view behind is even more spectacular – Derwentwater with the Skiddaw massif behind it.

King's How, which is owned by the National Trust, was named as a memorial to Kind Edward VII in 1910. The memorial plaque, close to the summit, states that the fell was dedicated by his sister Louise "as a sanctuary of rest and peace".

5. Retrace your steps as far as the cairn just after the memorial plaque. Now turn right to head steeply downhill. At the bottom of the drop, cross the stile in the fence. The path ahead isn't obvious at first, but soon becomes clearer. It crosses a ladder stile and then fords a tiny beck before climbing again. At the top of this climb, turn sharp left – almost heading back on yourself.

6. Keep to this path until you reach a clear fork. The one up to the left quickly climbs to the summit of Jopplety How, a good, semi-enclosed spot for lunch. The route then continues by returning to the fork and turning left. Having crossed a ladder stile, bear left. The path to Watendlath is unclear and boggy in places. The key is to follow the line of the wall that you can see over to your left until Watendlath Tarn appears below. The wall comes to an abrupt, temporary halt here, while the path, clearer now, keeps to the high ground before making its way down to a kissing-gate.

7. Beyond the gate, head straight down the grassy slope towards Watendlath. Turn left along the clear track and through the gate.

Watendlath is a tiny gathering of cottages and farms, clustered alongside a picturesque tarn. The drove road here was maintained by the monks of Furness Abbey to link Borrowdale with Wythburn. The hamlet first got mains electricity in 1978, the last place in the Lake District to be connected. The first telephone didn't arrive until 1984.

Watendlath was the setting for Hugh Walpole's 1931 novel

> Judith Paris. *It was the second of four novels belonging to the* Herries Chronicle. *Set in Keswick, Borrowdale, Watendlath, Uldale and Ireby, these books told the story of the Herries family from the 18th century to the depression of the 1930s.*

8. Do not cross the outlet stream (Watendlath Beck); instead, go through the gate beside the humpback bridge and follow the beck for 2km through the hanging valley.

> *Watendlath Beck, situated at about 220m above sea level, is one of Borrowdale's many hanging valleys. "Hanging" above the level of the glaciated valley floor (Borrowdale), it was gouged out by a tributary to the main glacier, and so didn't erode as deeply. The difference in levels is exaggerated by the Skiddaw slates of the main valley being eroded more quickly than the Borrowdale volcanics, on which the beck lies.*

9. When you reach a bridge over the beck, turn left to go through a kissing-gate. The path heads through the woods and down a rocky ravine. As you approach the bottom of this ravine, bear left along a faint path and then left again.

> *You should now be able to hear the higher of the Lodore Falls. This cataract marks the beginning of Watendlath's Beck's tumultuous plunge from its hanging valley into Borrowdale below.*

10. Go through one gate beside the waterfall and then a gap in a tumbledown wall to head downhill through the trees. The path drops back down on to the Borrowdale Road at High Lodore Farm. Turn left and the parking area is about 800 metres along the road.

Other titles by

QUESTA PUBLISHING LIMITED

LAKE DISTRICT
WALKS WITH CHILDREN
Buttermere and the Vale of Lorton
Around Coniston
Borrowdale
Ullswater
Around Kendal
Around Windermere
South Lakeland

EASY RAMBLES
Around Keswick and Borrowdale
Around Ambleside and Grasmere
Around Eskdale
Around Wasdale
Around Ennerdale & Calder Valley
Around Dunnerdale
Around Coniston and Hawkshead
Around Patterdale and Ullswater
Around the Langdale Valleys

SHORT WALKS
In the Lake District

YORKSHIRE DALES
WALKS WITH CHILDREN
Wharfedale
Swaledale
Wensleydale
Malham and Airedale
Ribblesdale

PEAK DISTRICT
WALKS WITH CHILDREN
Dark Peak

PENNINES
SHORT WALKS
Eden Valley and North Pennines

All QUESTA titles are available from
27 Camwood, Clayton-le-Woods,
BAMBER BRIDGE, Lancashire PR5 8LA, by FAX to
0705 349 1743, or email to sales@questapublishing.co.uk

www.questapublishing.co.uk